Flea

Karen Hartley,
Chris Macro,
and Philip Taylor

Heinemann Library
Chicago, Illinois

© 2000 Reed Educational & Professional Publishing
Published by Heinemann Library,
an imprint of Reed Educational & Professional Publishing,
Chicago, IL
Customer Service 888-454-2279
Visit our website at www.heinemannlibrary.com

Designed by Ron Kamen
Illustrated by Alan Fraser at Pennant Illustration
Originated by Ambassador Litho
Printed in China by South China Printing Co. Ltd.

04 03 02 01
10 9 8 7 6 5 4 3 2

Library of Congress Cataloging-in-Publication Data
Hartley, Karen, 1949-
    Flea / Karen Hartley, Chris Macro, Philip Taylor.
      p. cm. -- (Bug books)
    Includes bibliographical references (p.) and index.
    Summary: An introduction to fleas, including what they look like, how they are born, what they eat, how they grow, and where they live.
    ISBN 1-57572-547-9 (lib.bdg.)
    1. Fleas--Juvenile literature. [1. Fleas.] I. Macro, Chris, 1940- II. Taylor, Philip, 1949- III. Title. IV. Series.

QL599.5 .H37 2000
595.77'5--dc21   99-057443

Acknowledgments

The Publishers would like to thank the following for permission to reproduce photographs:
Oxford Scientific Films/Alastair MacEwen, p. 4; FLPA/Silvestris, p. 5; Bruce Coleman/Kim Taylor, p. 6; Science Photo Library/Eye of Science, p. 7; Ardea London/Bob Gibbons, pp. 8, 12; Science Photo Library/J.C. Revy, p. 9; Ardea London/John Mason, pp. 10, 11, 13; Science Photo Library/K.H. Kjeldsen, p. 14; Ardea London/John Clegg, p. 15; Ardea London/M. Watson, p. 16; Bubbles/Jacqui Farrow, p. 17; Tony Stone/Wayne R. Bilenduke, p. 18; Tony Stone/David Tipling, p. 19; Nature Phtographers Ltd./N.A. Callow, p. 20; Tony Stone/NHMPL, p. 21; London Scientific Films, p. 22; Ardea London/Stefan Meyers, p. 23; Oxford Scientific Films/G.I. Bernard, p. 24; Bruce Coleman/Hans Reinhard, p. 25; Heather Angel, p. 26; NHPA/Stephen Dalton, p. 27; Ardea London/Francois Gohier, p. 28; Planet Earth Pictures/Paulo De Oliveira, p. 29.

Cover photograph reproduced with permission of Peter Parks/Oxford Scientific Films.

Every effort has been made to contact copyright holders of any material reproduced in this book. Any omissions will be rectified in subsequent printings if notice is given to the Publisher.

Some words are shown in bold, **like this.** You can find out what they mean by looking in the glossary.

Contents

What Are Fleas?

Fleas are **insects**. There are about 2,000 different kinds of fleas in the world.

Fleas are called **parasites** because they live on other animals. Fleas live only on animals which are warm-blooded, like cats, dogs, sheep, and even humans.

What Fleas Look Like

Fleas have flat bodies that are shiny and hard. They have lots of sharp spines to keep them from sliding off animals' hair. Fleas are usually brown.

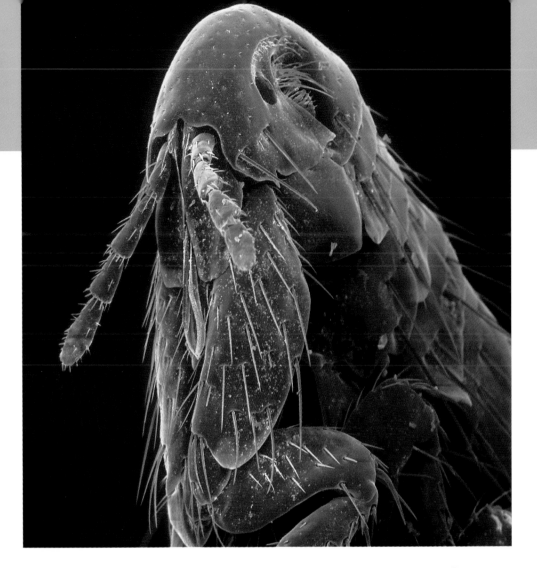

Fleas have two short **antennae** for smelling and feeling. Most fleas have large eyes, but some can only see shapes and tell when it is light or dark.

How Big Are Fleas?

Fleas that live on cats and dogs are smaller than the head of a pin. A flea that lives on a mole is one of the biggest kinds. It is about the size of a pea.

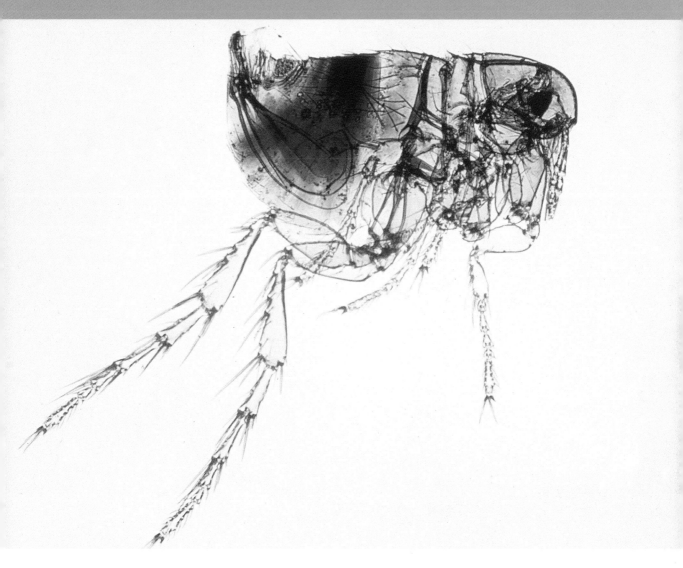

Fleas that live on people are bigger than cat and dog fleas, but they are still very tiny. They are a bit bigger than the head of a pin.

How Fleas Are Born

Female fleas lay tiny white eggs. Cat fleas can lay about 25 eggs a day for several weeks. The eggs may **hatch** after about five days.

The **larvae** that hatch from the eggs are long and pale. They do not have eyes or legs, but have tiny hairs on their bodies to help them wriggle around.

How Fleas Grow

Flea **larvae** eat dust and hairs from the **host** animal's sleeping place. They also need to feed on blood, which **adult** fleas pass on in their **droppings**.

As it grows, a larva **molts** two or three times. After a few weeks, the larva makes a **cocoon**. It is now called a **pupa**. The adult flea is ready to leave the cocoon after one or two weeks.

What Fleas Eat

A flea's mouth has a sharp, thin tube that it uses to stick into the **host** animal's skin and suck its blood. When fleas finish eating, they usually jump off the host animal, but some stay on.

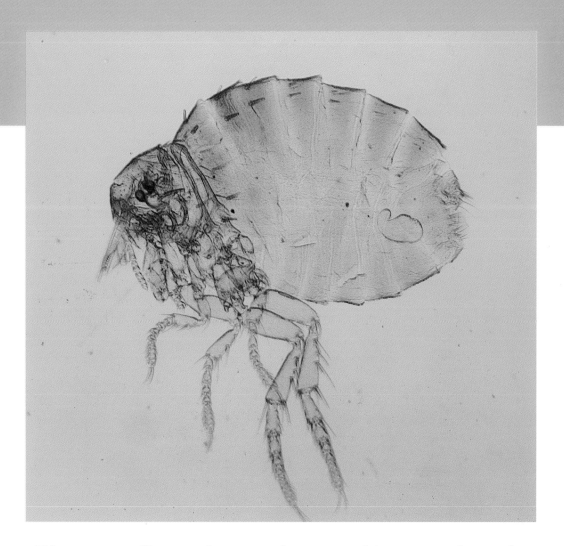

Chigger fleas bury themselves under the animal's skin and suck blood all the time. Chiggers can even bury themselves under people's skin!

Which Animals Attack Fleas?

Flea **larvae** are fierce **predators**. They will kill and eat **adult** fleas that are weak. **Host** animals try to get rid of fleas by scratching themselves.

Fleas are **pests,** so people try to kill
them with special powders and sprays.
When people **vacuum** their carpets,
they suck up the eggs and larvae.

Where Fleas Live

Most fleas live in countries where it is not too hot and not too cold. But some fleas can live in very cold places, like the Arctic or Antarctica.

Some fleas can live on people, but most live on animals like cats, dogs, rabbits, and moles. Some fleas live on birds. Fleas also live where animals sleep.

How Fleas Move

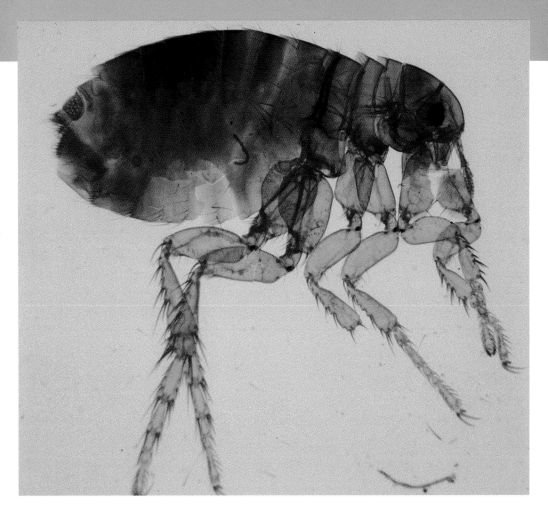

Fleas' bodies have three main parts.
The middle part has three pairs of legs.
Stiff, sharp hairs on their legs help the
fleas cling to an animal's fur or hair.

Fleas do not have wings, so they jump onto the **host** animal. Their back legs are very strong. Some fleas can jump up to 200 times their own height!

How Long Fleas Live

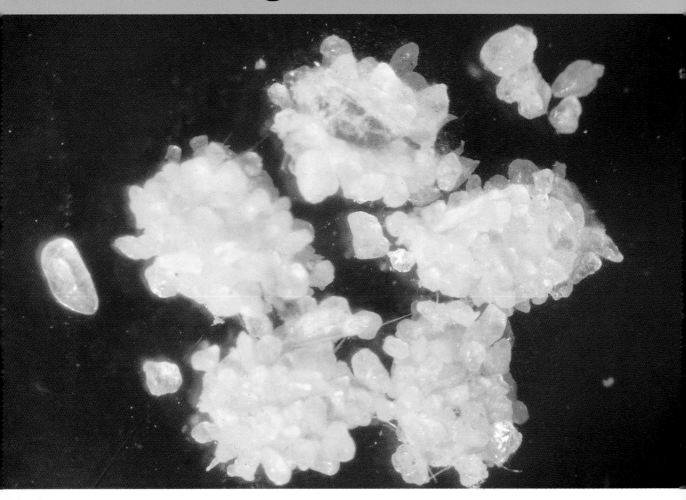

If it is cold, fleas can stay in their **cocoons** for much longer than one or two weeks. When a flea does come out of its cocoon, it will live for about six months.

Most fleas can live on different animals, but some live on just one kind. Rabbit fleas can only feed on rabbit blood, so if there are no **host** rabbits, the fleas die.

What Fleas Do

When fleas suck blood, they put **saliva** into the bite. The saliva is special because it keeps the blood flowing while the flea is sucking. It makes the bite itch afterwards.

If a flea sucks blood from an animal that is sick, it makes the next animal it bites sick, too. This cat is wearing a special collar that keeps fleas from biting it.

How Are Fleas Special?

Fleas can live without food for a long time. If the **host** animal dies or leaves its sleeping place, the fleas have time to look for another host.

If there is no host animal when a flea is ready to leave its **cocoon**, it will stay inside and wait. When an animal comes near, the flea feels the movement or its body heat and jumps on!

Thinking about Fleas

Dinosaurs lived a very long time ago. They had thick, tough skin and no fur. Fleas did not live on dinosaurs. Can you think why?

Fleas are able to jump very high. Some can even somersault in midair. Can you remember how their long, strong legs help them to jump high?

Bug Map

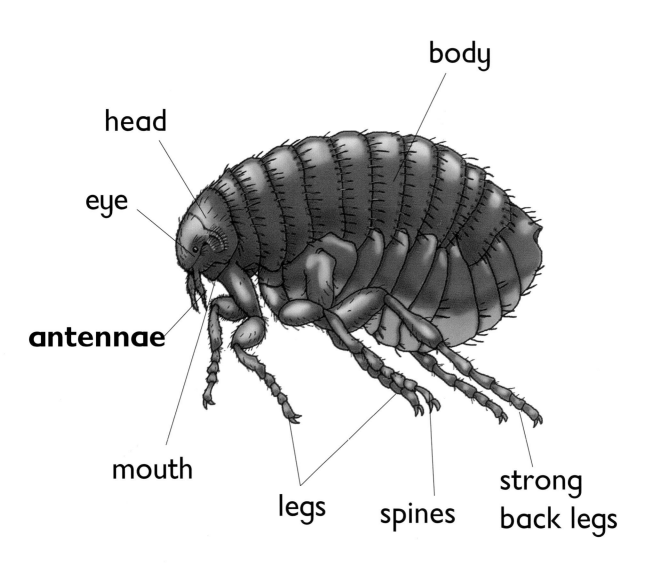

body

head

eye

antennae

mouth

legs

spines

strong
back legs

Glossary

adult grown-up

antenna (more than one are antennae) thin tube on an insect's head that may be used to smell, feel, or hear

cocoon silky bag that a larva makes around itself

dropping body waste from an animal

hatch to come out of an egg

host animal on which a flea feeds

insect small animal with six legs

larva (more than one are larvae) baby insect that hatches from an egg

molt to shed an old skin that is too small

parasite animal that lives on another kind of animal

pest animal that bothers people

predator animal that hunts another animal

pupa (more than one are pupae) stage of an insect's life during which it turns into an adult

saliva liquid made in the mouths of many animals; spit

vacuum to suck up dirt using a special machine

More Books to Read

Fisher, Enid. *Fleas.* Milwaukee: Gareth Stevens, Inc., 1997.

Stevenson, Kathy. *Fleas.* Chanhassen, Minn.: The Child's World, Inc., 1999.

Index